Chicken's Made Of Chicken

Written and Illustrated by Mic Fox

Please write Famly LLC at fortfamly.com

ISBN 9781721147885

for my Violent Vegans
and my Considerate Carnivores.
Your irony is unmatched.

The cow, the fish, the pig, and the chicken
all live on the farm.

And everyday, at 12-o-clock,
the lunch bell does alarm.

Once a month the farmer
and his buddies get together.

They set up tables, bring some food,
and share it–pending weather.

But when everybody's having fun
and the farmer isn't looking,

the animals sneak out of their pens
and feast on all the cooking.

Most of the animals fill their plates
with the veggies they've been pickin'.

But one day someone grabbed the meat.
That someone was the chicken!

The animals stared in silence.
They were shocked by the chicken's platter!

And one by one they confronted him
about this crazy matter.

But the chicken paid no minds.
He laughed in carnivoric bliss.

And then he gorged himself
on all the meats
and shook his chicken fist.

"Oh how I love this BURGER!"

"But that burger's made of COW!"

"Well, I'm gonna eat this burger.
And I'm gonna eat it NOW!"

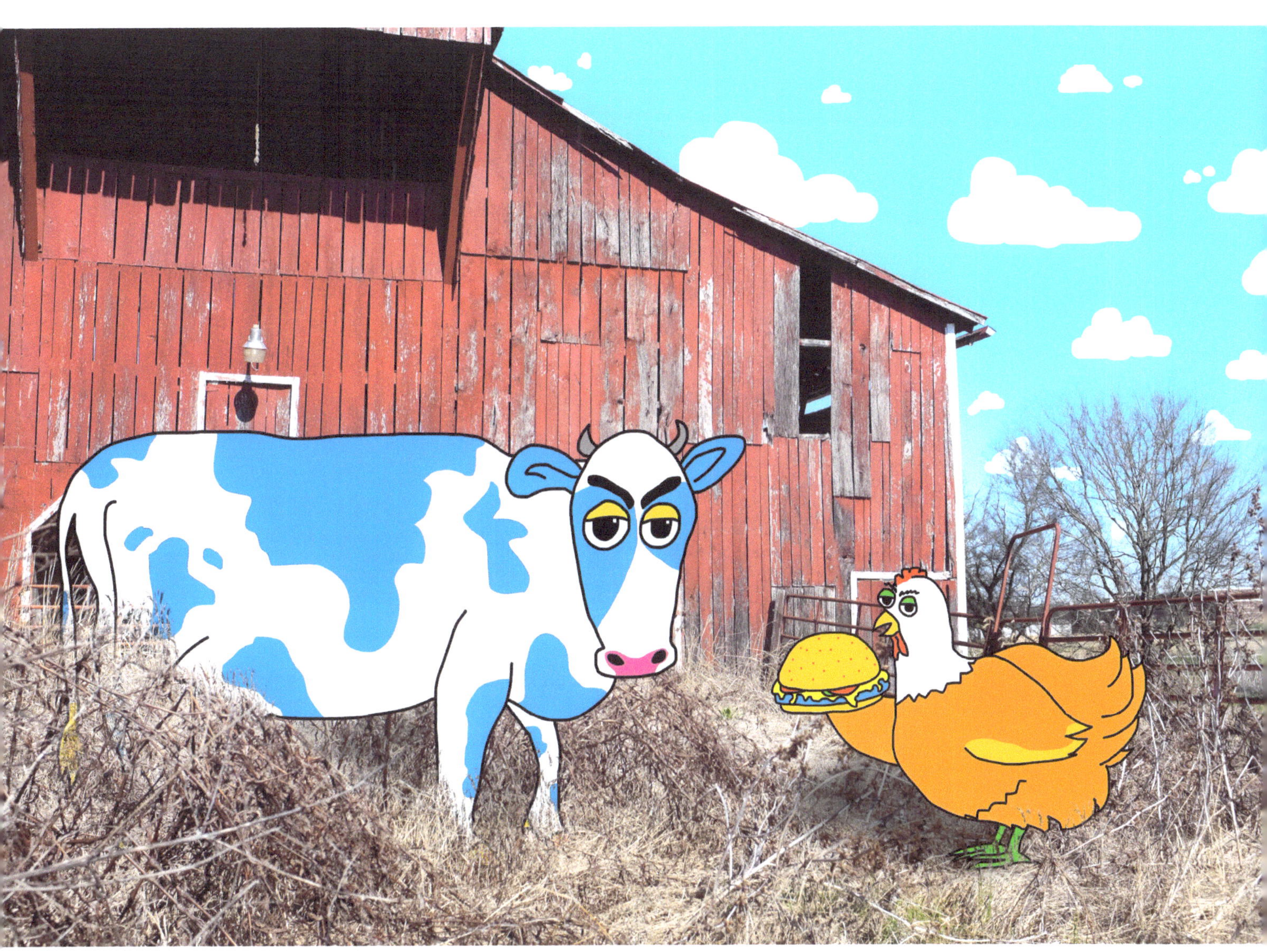

"I want to eat some SUSHI!"

"But the sushi's made of FISH!
And chickens don't eat SUSHI!"

"But this sushi is DELISH!"

"I want to eat this SAUSAGE!"

"Isn't sausage made of PIG?!"

"Well, when you cover it with
sauce, you know that
PIG is what I DIG!"

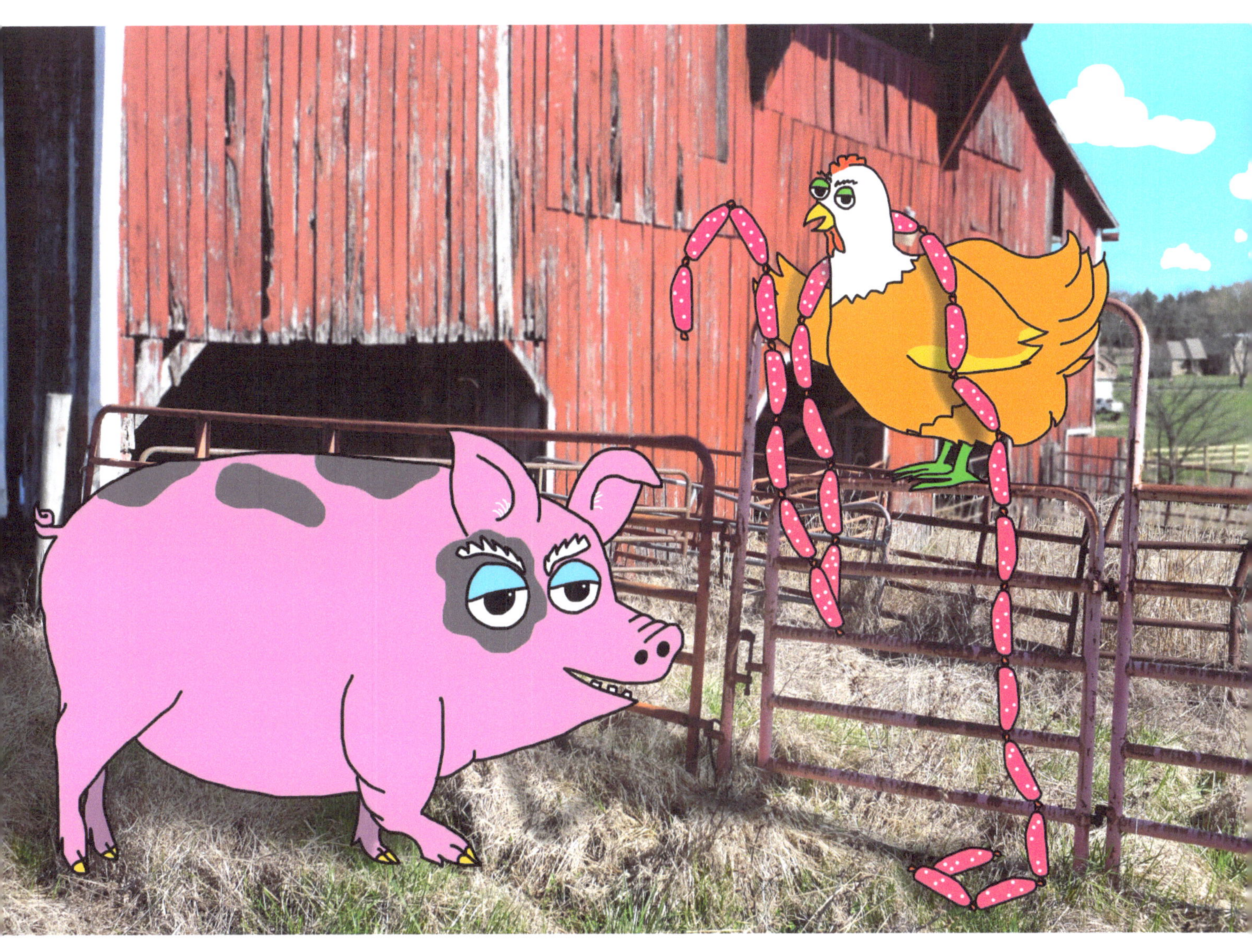

"We gotta get together.
The chicken's acting like a jerk."

"Yeah, I think he wants to eat us."

"I've got something
that could work."

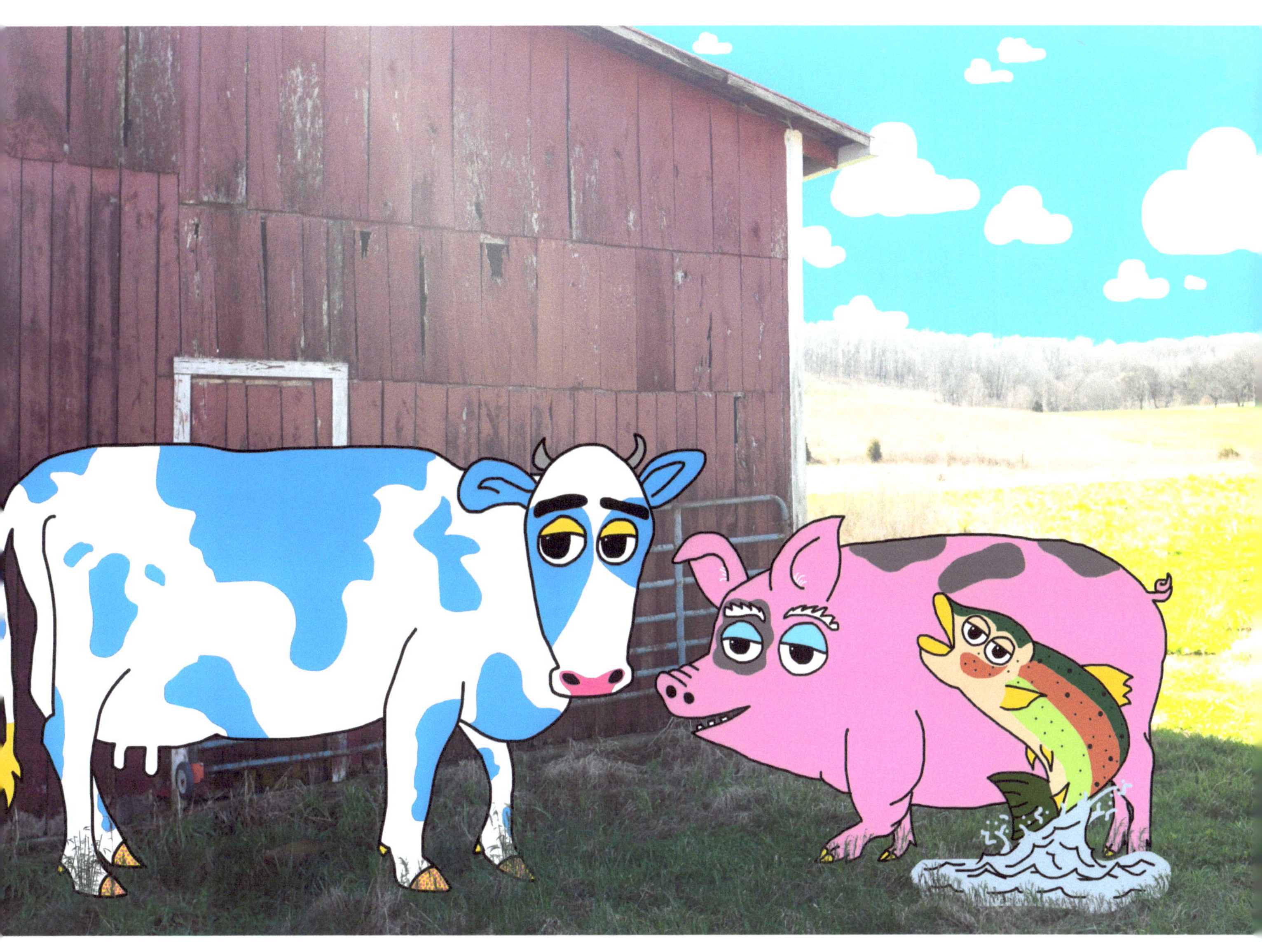

"Hey CHICKEN!
We don't like you snacking
on all of our friends.

If you'd be so kind to stop it,
I'm sure we could make amends."

"But all you guys are tastey!
You're so tender and so sweet!
I've tasted COW and FISH and PIG;
You know the taste just can't be beat!"

"Well have you tried
the
CHICKEN?"

"NO!

'Cause chicken's
made of...

CHICKEN!"

"Well, if you grill it up or fry it,

it's the CHICKEN I'll be pickin!"

And all of the sudden the chicken, well...
was no longer a burden.
The cow, the fish, and pig then got
the peace they'd been deservin'.

Rumor has it, the chicken went to
visit some friends, upstate.
Either that or he ended up getting fried
and put on someone's plate.